With thoughts of

Ann Kellam Bott

GREAT AMERICAN SHORT STORIES

Mark Twain

Stories retold by Prescott Hill

Illustrated by Tracy Hall

GARETH**STEVENS**
GS
PUBLISHING
A World Almanac Education Group Company

Please visit our web site at: www.garethstevens.com
For a free color catalog describing Gareth Stevens Publishing's
list of high-quality books and multimedia programs, call
1-800-542-2595 (USA) or 1-800-387-3178 (Canada).
Gareth Stevens Publishing's fax: (414) 332-3567.

Library of Congress Cataloging-in-Publication Data

Hill, Prescott.
    Mark Twain / stories retold by Prescott Hill; illustrated by Tracy Hall.
      p. cm. — (Great American short stories)
    Summary: Adaptations of five humorous tales by Mark Twain, plus an introduction
to the author and discussion questions.
    Contents: The celebrated jumping frog of Calaveras County—The Californian's tale—
The professor's yarn—The million-pound bank note—A fable.
    ISBN 0-8368-4255-3 (lib. bdg.)
    1. Children's stories, American. [1. Humorous stories. 2. Short stories.]
I. Twain, Mark, 1835–1910. II. Hall, Tracy, ill. III. Title. IV. Series.
PZ7.H557217Mar 2004
[Fic]—dc22
                                     2004045214

This North American hardcover edition published in 2005 with the
permission of AGS Publishing exclusively by
Gareth Stevens Publishing
A World Almanac Education Group Company
330 West Olive Street, Suite 100
Milwaukee, WI 53212 USA

Gareth Stevens editor: Barbara Kiely Miller
Gareth Stevens cover and text design: Steve Schraenkler
Gareth Stevens picture researcher: Diane Laska-Swanke

Cover Photo: © Mansell/Time Life Pictures/Getty Images

Printed in the United States of America

1 2 3 4 5 6 7 8 9 08 07 06 05 04

CONTENTS

Introduction

*"The universe is made of
stories, not atoms."*
—Muriel Rukeyser

"The story's about you."
—Horace

Everyone loves a good story. It is hard
to think of a friendlier introduction to
classic literature. For one thing, short
stories are *short*—quick to get into and
easy to finish. Of all the literary forms,
the short story is the least intimidating
and the most approachable.

Great literature is an important part of
our human heritage. In the belief that
this heritage belongs to everyone, the
Great American Short Stories series is
adapted for today's readers. Lengthy
sentences and paragraphs are shortened.
Archaic words are replaced. Modern
punctuation and spellings are used. Many
of the longer stories are abridged. In all
the stories, painstaking care has been

taken to preserve the author's unique voice.

Great American Short Stories has something for everyone. The stories in the collection cover a broad terrain of themes, story types, and styles. Literary merit was a deciding factor in story selection. But no story was included unless it was as enjoyable as it was instructive. And special priority was given to stories that shine light on the human condition.

Each book in the *Great American Short Stories* series is devoted to the work of a single author. Little-known stories of merit are included with famous, old favorites. Taken as a whole, the collected authors and stories make up a rich and diverse sampler of the storyteller's art.

Great American Short Stories guarantees a great reading experience. Readers who look for common interests, concerns, and experiences are sure to find them. Readers who bring their own gifts of perception and appreciation to the stories will be doubly rewarded.

❦ Mark Twain ❧
(1835–1910)

About the Author

Mark Twain was a charming, natural–born storyteller who cared little for form or rules of style. One of his biographers described his talent in these words: "What he had was the naked power of the man with the gift of gab. He knew what a yarn was, and what it was for, and what to do with it."

Born Samuel Langhorne Clemens, he grew up in the busy port city of Hannibal, Missouri. This became the setting for his two most famous books, *The Adventures of Tom Sawyer* and *The Adventures of Huckleberry Finn*, his masterpiece.

Young Clemens was just twelve when his father died. Before becoming a writer, he worked as a printer's apprentice and a steamboat pilot. At the age of twenty-eight he chose his famous pen name. The words *mark twain* mean "two fathoms deep." It was a term used to measure the depth of the water from a riverboat.

In many ways, Twain was more of a journalist and an entertainer than a "serious" short-story writer. His great gifts were humor, the common touch, and the ability to imitate any style of speech. It was said that he wrote very rapidly and was as proud as a boy of his daily turnout.

Twain had a very long and happy marriage. After his wife's death, he wrote a story about Adam and Eve. In it, after Eve dies, Adam says, "Wherever she was, *there* was Eden."

Twain's influence on the writers that came after him has been enormous. Even today he stands as a solid monument in American literature. If you like hearing a good story from a man who loved to tell one, you can't help but enjoy Mark Twain.

The Celebrated Jumping Frog of Calaveras County

How far would you go to win a bet? This funny story is one of Mark Twain's most famous. Although it reads like a spoof or a tall tale, it is not. The plot was based on an actual event reported in California newspapers.

"HE CAN OUTJUMP ANY FROG IN CALAVERAS COUNTY!"

The Celebrated Jumping Frog of Calaveras County

A friend wrote me from the East. He asked me to visit old Simon Wheeler. The purpose was to ask Wheeler about my friend's friend, Leonidas W. Smiley.

I did visit Wheeler. But now I wonder if there really is a *Leonidas* W. Smiley at all. I think maybe my friend wanted me to remind Wheeler of *Jim* Smiley. Or maybe he wanted Wheeler to bore me to death with some story about Jim Smiley. Maybe he knew that such a story would be long, tedious, and useless to me. If that was his plan, it succeeded.

I found Simon Wheeler sleeping by the barroom stove of a run-down tavern. The town was called Angel's Camp, and it was in California. It was a decaying old gold-mining town. Right away I noticed that Wheeler was fat and bald-headed. But the sleeping man had a simple, gentle look.

He woke up and said hello. I told him that a friend of mine wanted to know about Leonidas W. Smiley.

Simon Wheeler backed me into a corner and blocked my way with his chair. Then he told me the story I am about to tell you. He never smiled, he never frowned, he never changed his voice. He did not tell the story as if it were funny or odd in any way. He seemed to think it was an important matter. And he clearly thought its two heroes were geniuses. So I just let him talk. I never interrupted him once.

"I don't know about any *Leonidas*," he began. "But I knew a feller name of *Jim* Smiley. He came to Angel's Camp a few years back. I remember that he would bet on anything—if he could find someone to bet on the other side. If he couldn't, he'd change sides. Any way that suited the other man, suited *him*. He was happy just so long as he got to bet at all.

"He'd bet on horse races. He'd bet on dog fights. If there was two birds setting on a fence, he'd bet you which one would fly first. He'd bet on anything.

"Once, Parson Walker's wife was very sick. For a while, everyone feared she might die. When Smiley saw the Parson, he asked how his wife was doing. The Parson said that she was doing better. It looked like she would pull through after all. Before he thought twice, Smiley said, 'I'll bet you two dollars she doesn't.'

"Smiley had a horse. The boys called her the fifteen-minute nag, because she ran so slow. But he used to win money betting on her, even though she was usually sick. They used to give her a big head start. The other horses would pass her at first. But by the end of the race, she'd catch up. She'd come along kicking and coughing and sneezing—but she'd end up about a neck ahead of the others.

"And he had a little bulldog that didn't look worth a cent. But as soon as Smiley made a bet on him, he became different. A big dog might throw him around, but the little bulldog wouldn't quit. Finally, when Smiley had made all the bets he could, the little dog would start in. He would grab the other dog's hind leg in his teeth. Then he would just hang on to it until the other dog gave up.

"Andrew Jackson was the dog's name, and Smiley always won money betting on him. But then one day the little dog fought a dog that didn't *have* any hind legs. They'd been sawed off in an accident. When Andrew Jackson saw that, he didn't know what to do. He didn't have anything to grab onto. He looked at Smiley like it was his fault. How could he have matched him with a dog with no hind legs? That was the day that little dog just quit. He walked away and lay down and died.

"One day, Smiley caught a frog and took him home to educate him. For three months he sat in the backyard, teaching that frog to jump. Dan'l Webster was that frog's name. Smiley got him so he could jump in the air and turn somersaults. And the frog would always land on his feet— just like a cat. He could jump better than any frog around.

"Smiley kept him in a little box and took him into town sometimes. One day a stranger came into Angel's Camp. He asked Smiley what was in the box. 'It might be a parrot,' Smiley said, 'or it might be a canary. But it ain't. It's only just a frog.'

"The stranger looked at the frog and said, 'What's he good for?'

"'He can outjump any frog in Calaveras County,' Smiley boasted.

"The man said he couldn't see anything special about the frog.

"'Maybe *you* don't,' Smiley said, 'but I've got *my* opinion. I'll bet forty dollars he can outjump any frog in Calaveras County.'

"'Well,' the stranger said, 'I don't have a frog.'

"'That's all right,' Smiley said. 'If you hold my box, I'll go get you one.' Then he handed the stranger the box and dashed off to find another frog.

"While Smiley was gone, the man took Dan'l Webster out of the box. He held open the frog's mouth and filled him full of quail shot. You know—those little BBs you find in shotgun shells. He filled that poor frog pretty near up to his chin.

"In a little bit, Smiley came back with a frog in his hand. He gave the frog to the stranger. 'Now, if you're ready, set him next to Dan'l,' he said.

"The two men put their frogs on the ground and touched them from behind. The new frog hopped off, very lively. Dan'l just moved his shoulders hard. He couldn't seem to move off the ground.

"The stranger took the money and started away. But he stopped for a moment and pointed at Dan'l Webster. 'I don't see that that frog's much better than any other,' he said. Then he left for good.

"Smiley scratched his head and looked at his frog. He picked him up and noticed he seemed pretty heavy. When Smiley tipped him a little bit, the quail shot started pouring out of Dan'l Webster's mouth. Then Smiley guessed what the stranger had done. He was the maddest man you ever saw. He took off after the stranger, but he never caught him. And—"

Just then, Simon Wheeler heard his name being called from the front yard. He got up to see what was wanted. As he moved away he turned to me and said, "Wait. Just set where you are and rest easy. I'll only be gone for a second."

But I didn't think any more talk of *Jim* Smiley would give me much information about *Leonidas* W. Smiley. I headed off.

At the door I met Wheeler just as he was coming back.

"Well," he said, "one time this Smiley had a yellow, one-eyed cow that didn't have a tail. It just had a short stump like a banana—"

But I had grown tired of his stories. I had no time and no wish to hear about the poor cow. I took my leave.

The Californian's Tale

Did all of the gold-diggers "strike it rich" in California's gold rush? The fact is that most of the prospectors went home empty-handed. Some didn't go home at all. This tender story is about the brotherhood that grew between the unlucky.

"THAT PICTURE WAS TAKEN THE DAY WE WERE MARRIED. WHEN YOU SEE HER—OH, JUST WAIT UNTIL YOU SEE HER!"

The Californian's Tale

About thirty-five years ago, I was prospecting for gold near the Stanislaus River in California. All day long I tramped around with pick and pan. I was always expecting to strike it rich, although I never did.

It was lovely country. Once there had been a lot of people there—but they had left when the gold ran out. There had even been a little city there at one time. It had banks, newspapers, a fire station, and a mayor. But all that was long gone. Now there was nothing left but a green meadow.

Not far from there you could still find pretty little houses covered with vines and roses. They were empty now. The families that lived there during the gold rush had left them behind. They couldn't sell them or give them away.

Farther down the road, you could find a few old log cabins from the mining days. Some of the men who built them still lived there. Most were there because they had not struck it rich. They were ashamed to go home to wherever they came from. For years they had not kept in touch with their families or old friends. At age forty, they were living dead men. They felt they had wasted their lives.

It was a lonesome place, with few people around for company. There was nothing there to make a man feel glad to be alive. And so, one afternoon, I was grateful to see a human creature. He was a man about forty-five years old. I saw him standing at the gate of a little, rose-covered house. Somehow it didn't look empty like the others. Its front yard was filled with pretty flowers. Someone was taking good care of it.

The man invited me in and told me to make myself at home.

It was a delight to be in a real home after long weeks of prospecting. The cheerful nest made me as happy as a hungry man who had been given a good meal.

There was a colorful rag carpet and pretty wallpaper. There were framed pictures on the walls, a clean cloth on the table, and vases of flowers around the room. There were many other little touches that only a woman's hand could bring.

My happiness showed on my face.

The man smiled at me. "It's all *her* work," he said. "She did it all herself— every bit." He looked about the room with pride. Then he went over to a chair that was draped with a piece of silk. The hang of the silk didn't seem right to him, so he patted it and smoothed it out.

"She always does that," he said to me. "You can't tell just what it lacks. But it does lack something until you've done that. You can see after you've done it—but you can't tell just what it is. There's no rules to it. It's like the finishing pats a mother gives after brushing her child's hair. I've seen her fix all these things so much, I can do it her way. I still don't understand it all. She knows the hows and whys. I just understand how."

He showed me the bedroom. There were white pillows, a carpeted floor, a dressing table with a mirror, and little perfume bottles. The bathroom was clean and neat. There were fancy soaps and clean white towels. I smiled again.

"All her work," he said. "She did it all herself—every bit. There's nothing here that hasn't felt the touch of her hand. Now wouldn't you think—but I mustn't talk so much."

I looked about, glancing at one detail after another. I felt there was something special that he wanted me to see. For some reason, though, he wanted me to discover it for myself. I looked all around, still not knowing what I was looking for. Then I saw that I was looking right at it. He broke into a happy laugh and rubbed his hands together.

"That's *it*!" he said. "You've found it! I knew you would. It's her picture."

I went to the dresser and picked it up. It showed the sweetest, most beautiful face I had ever seen. The man smiled to see the look on my face.

"She was nineteen her last birthday," he said, putting the picture back on the dresser. "That picture was taken the day we were married. When you see her—oh, just wait until you see her!"

"Where is she?" I asked. "When will she be back?"

"Oh, she's away now. She's gone to see her family. They live about fifty miles from here. She's been gone two weeks today."

"When do you expect her?" I asked.

"This is Wednesday. She'll be back Saturday night, about nine o'clock."

"I'm sorry," I said, "but I'll be gone by then."

"Gone?" he cried. "No! Why should

you go? *Don't go.* She'll be so disappointed. You see, she likes to have people visit us. She loves to talk about everything. She knows so much! She reads so many books—you'd be surprised. Don't go. It's only a little while, and she'll be so disappointed."

He picked up the picture again and held it before me. "There now," he said, "tell it to her face. You could have stayed to see her, but you wouldn't."

That second look at her decided it. I would stay for a few more days.

That night he and I talked until late, mostly about his wife.

On Thursday evening, a big miner walked to the house from three miles away. "I just stopped by to ask about the little lady," he said. "When is she coming home? Is there any news from her?"

"Oh, yes," the man said, "would you like me to read you her letter, Tom?"

"Yes, I would, Henry," Tom said, "if you don't mind."

Henry got the letter out. He said he would skip some of the private things. It was a charming letter. In it she sent best wishes to Tom, and Joe, and Charley, and their other close friends.

When Henry had finished reading, he looked over at Tom. "Oh, you're at it again!" he cried out. "Take your hands away and let me see your eyes. You always do that when I read a letter from her. I will write and tell her."

"Oh, no," Tom said, "you mustn't, Henry. I'm getting old, you know. Any little disappointment makes me want to cry. I thought she'd be here herself—and now you've only got a letter."

"Well, what put that in your head?" Henry said. "I thought everyone knew she wouldn't be home until Saturday."

"Saturday!" Tom said. "Come to think of it, I *did* know that. Well, I must be going. But I'll be on hand when she comes back."

Late Friday another old miner stopped by. He said the boys wanted to have a little party for her Saturday night. Did Henry think she'd be too tired for that?

"Tired!" Henry said. "Joe, you know

she'd stay up six weeks just to please any one of you!"

Then Joe asked about the letter, and Henry read it to him. After Henry finished, Joe said, "Lord, we miss her so!"

Saturday afternoon I kept looking at my watch. Henry noticed. "Do you think she'll be back so early?" he said.

I said I didn't think so, and laughed. I told him that looking at my watch was just a habit. But that didn't satisfy him. He went out four times to look for her.

"I'm getting worried," he said. "I know she's not due home until nine o'clock. Still, I worry about her. You don't think anything has happened to her?"

I said no.

He asked again a little later, and I said no again. Just then Charley, another miner, stopped by. He asked Henry to read the letter to him, and Henry did.

Pretty soon Tom and Joe arrived. We all set about decorating the house with flowers. Toward nine o'clock the three miners brought out their musical instruments. They had a fiddle, a banjo, and a clarinet. They started to play some lively tunes.

When it was almost nine o'clock, Henry stood in the doorway looking out at the road.

Joe brought out a tray with filled glasses for us all. He took one for himself, and Tom and Charley each took one. As I started to take a glass, Joe growled at me, "Not that one. Take the other."

I did as he said. Henry took the last one, and we all drank a toast to her arrival.

Henry had just swallowed his drink when the clock began to strike. His face grew pale. "Boys," he said, "I'm sick with fear. Help me—I want to lie down."

They helped him to the couch. He began to get drowsy. Then he said—as though talking in his sleep—"Did I hear horses' feet? Have they come?"

Tom leaned close to Henry. "It's just Jimmy Parrish. He says she'll be here in another half hour."

"Oh," Henry said, "I'm so glad nothing

has happened."

And then he fell into deep sleep. In a moment the miners undressed him and put him into bed. Then they got ready to leave the house.

"Wait," I said. "Don't go. She won't know me. I am a stranger."

They looked at each other. Then Joe said, "She? Poor thing, she's been dead for nineteen years!"

"Dead?" I said.

"Yes," Joe said. "She went to see her family a few months after she and Henry were married. On the way back she was killed in an Indian attack."

"And he lost his mind because of that?" I asked.

"Yes," Joe said, "He has never been sane since then. But he only gets bad when this time of year comes around. Then we all drop in to watch him. Three days before she's due, we come by and start talking about her. Then on Saturday we get things ready for a party.

"The first time there were twenty-seven of us. Now there's just the three. We always put something in his drink to make him sleep—or he would go wild. But then he's all right for another year. He thinks she's with him—until the last three or four days come round. Then he gets out his poor old letter. And we come and ask him to read it to us. Lord, she was a darling!"

The Professor's Yarn

Have you ever tried to trick someone and ended up by getting tricked yourself? This shipboard adventure takes place on a trip from New York to California. One of the passengers appears to be a bore and a fool. But is he really what he seems to be?

"THE MONEY WOULD JUST ROLL IN, I PROMISE YOU.
AND OF COURSE I'D GIVE YOU A GOOD SHARE OF IT."

The Professor's Yarn

It was in the early days before I was a college professor. I was but a young land surveyor then, and I had a contract to work in California.

As this story begins, I was on my way there by sea—a voyage of three or four weeks. There were many passengers on board, but I had little to say to them. In those days, I was mostly interested in reading and thinking, so I didn't talk much to other people.

There were three professional gamblers on board—rough, repulsive fellows. I never talked with them at all, but I saw them often. They gambled in one of the ship's cabins day and night. I often passed that cabin during my walks about the ship. The door was always ajar—to let out the blue clouds of tobacco smoke and swearing. I knew they were an evil and hateful bunch, but I had to put up with them, of course.

There was one passenger that I saw often. He wanted to be friends with me. I didn't know how to get rid of him without hurting his feelings. His name was John Backus, and I guessed from looking at him that he was a farmer. I thought that maybe he came from the backwoods of some state like Ohio. Later, he told me he raised cattle in that very state. I was so pleased to have guessed right that I took a liking to him.

Every day after breakfast we walked about the ship. He talked a lot about his business, his family, his relatives, his politics. He also managed to get me to tell him about *my* life. I guess he was good at it, for I don't usually talk much about myself.

How he liked to talk about cattle! His
eyes would light up at the bare name of
a bull or a cow. He knew all breeds, and
he loved all breeds. On that subject his
tongue would turn itself loose.

One day he invited me to come to his
cabin. He said that he needed to talk to
me about something. When we got there,
he said, "I've got an idea that might
interest you. It could be good for both of
us. You're not going to California for
fun—and neither am I. It's business,
right? Well, I've saved my money for
many years, and I've got it all here."

He held up a heavy cloth bag. "There's
ten thousand dollars in this bag," he said.
"Now here's my idea. I know a lot about
raising cattle. And I know that California
is just the place to do it. Well, when you
do your surveying, there's a special way
you can draw the lines. You could make it
so that little pieces of land are left over
that don't belong to anybody. Then I
could buy cattle and raise them on those
little pieces of land. For free of course.
The money would roll in, I promise you.

And of course I'd give you a good share of it."

I was sorry to say anything against his plan, but it could not be helped. "I am not that kind of surveyor," I said. "Let's change the subject, Mr. Backus."

He apologized at once. Clearly, he didn't think there was a thing wrong with his plan. But he seemed confused and embarrassed just the same.

We were stopped at Acapulco at the time. The ship's crew happened to be loading cattle. They were lifting the heavy animals with big rope slings. "Look at that!" Mr. Backus cried. "My goodness, what *would* they say about that back in Ohio?"

All the passengers were on deck, even the gamblers. Backus had talked to them all—everybody knew that his pet topic was raising cattle. As I moved away, the three gamblers went over to Backus. They talked for a while. Then I heard Backus say, "It's no use, gentlemen. I've told you a half-dozen times before—I'm not going to risk it."

I felt relieved. "His level head will protect him from those gamblers," I thought.

But the gamblers kept at him for the whole two-week trip from there to San Francisco. I warned him to stay away from them.

"Oh, yes," he said. "They want me to play cards with them. But I know better than to do that."

At last, we had almost reached San Francisco. It was a dark night, and I was on deck alone. As I took my evening walk, I saw a man leave the gamblers' cabin. I was shocked—for I was sure it was Backus. I started after him, but then lost him. I returned to the deck just in time to see him go back into the gamblers' cabin.

What was he doing? Had he gone to his cabin to get his bag of money?

The door to the gamblers' cabin was ajar. I looked in and there was Backus at the table, playing cards! Worse, he was drinking wine. The others made sure his glass was always full. The ship was in

San Francisco Harbor now. My only hope was that we would land before they cheated him out of all his money.

I watched as the dealer gave the players their cards. Backus drained his glass, picked up his cards, and smiled.

The three others pretended not to notice.

"How many cards do you want?" the dealer asked.

"None!" said Backus.

One of the professional gamblers, a fellow named Hank Wiley, threw down one card. The others each discarded three. Then the betting began. Backus started with a bet of ten dollars.

Hank Wiley raised the bet by twenty dollars. At that, the two other gamblers dropped out of the game. But Backus stayed in. Now he raised the bet by *fifty* dollars.

Wiley said, "I'll raise it a *hundred*!" He reached for the pile of money in the middle of the table. Guessing that Backus would drop out of he game, he started to laugh.

"Leave it alone," said Backus. "I'll raise it *another* hundred."

"Well, I'll raise it *five* hundred," said Wiley.

The betting went back and forth until there was ten thousand dollars at stake. Then Wiley put a bag of money on the table. "Here's five thousand more," he said to Backus. "What do you say to that?"

Backus put his own money bag on the table. "I call you," he said to Wiley. "What have you got?"

"Four kings, you fool!" said Wiley. He showed his cards and reached for the money.

"Four aces, you donkey!" shouted Backus. Then he drew out a pistol and kept the three gamblers covered. "*I am a professional gambler myself*" he said. "*I've been waiting to get at you three for this whole trip.*"

Just then the ship anchored and the trip was over.

Well it's a sad world. The dealer was Backus' "pal." The other two gamblers thought the dealer was going to cheat. He had agreed with them to give Backus four queens. But he crossed them up and gave Backus the winning hand.

A week later, I ran into Backus in San Francisco. He was dressed in the height of fashion. As we parted he said, "By the way, don't worry about that surveying idea I mentioned. I don't really know anything about cattle. I just picked up some facts from a farmer the day before we set sail. My interest in cattle-raising has served its turn—I won't be needing it anymore."

The Million-Pound Bank Note

A young American is broke and hungry when he arrives in London. In just a few short weeks he has become a millionaire—without working even a single day. What strange events turned his life around?

THE BROTHERS WONDERED WHAT WOULD
HAPPEN IF A STRANGER IN LONDON HAD JUST
THAT BANK NOTE AND NOTHING ELSE.

The Million-Pound Bank Note

When I was twenty-seven years old, I worked for a stock brokerage in San Francisco. I was alone in the world. All I had to depend on were my wits and a clean reputation. I felt that would be enough to earn me success.

On Saturday afternoons my time was my own. I liked to spend it sailing on a little boat in San Francisco Bay. One day I sailed too far and was carried out to sea. About nightfall, when I had lost all hope, a small ship rescued me. It was headed for London.

It was a long and stormy voyage. They made me work without pay for my passage. When I stepped ashore in London, my clothes were ragged and shabby. I had only a dollar in my pocket. That was enough to feed and shelter me for twenty-four hours. Then, for the next twenty-four hours, I went without food and shelter.

About ten o'clock the next morning, I was dragging myself along Portland Street. Suddenly I stopped. I saw a child throwing a half-eaten pear into the gutter. My mouth began to water. My stomach craved that pear—my whole being begged for it. But every time I started toward it, a few people came along. I would pretend that I wasn't interested in the pear. After they passed, I'd start for it again. Then someone else would come along. This same thing kept happening. Finally, I was ready to forget about shame and grab the pear. But just then, from a window behind me, I heard a voice. "Step in here, please," the voice said.

A butler let me into the building. He took me to a beautifully furnished room where two old gentlemen were sitting. They sent the butler away and asked me to sit down. I could see that they had just finished breakfast. The sight of the leftover food almost overpowered me.

Something had happened there that I knew nothing about. The two men were brothers. A couple of days before they'd had a pretty hot argument. Then they had made a bet to settle the matter.

The Bank of England had once issued two bank notes worth a million pounds each. One of them was used in a business deal with a foreign company. The other was never used. It was still in the vault at the Bank of England.

The brothers had been talking about that bank note. They wondered what would happen if a stranger in London had just that bank note and nothing else. They decided this stranger would have to be poor, honest, and smart. And there were other conditions. The stranger could have no friends in London. He could have no way to explain how he got hold of the bank note.

What would happen to him? Would he survive?

Brother A said the man would starve to death.

Brother B said he wouldn't.

Brother A said the man couldn't cash the note at a bank, because he would be arrested.

The two men argued for some time. Finally, Brother B made a bet with Brother A. He bet twenty thousand pounds that the man could live for at least thirty days on that million—and stay out of jail.

Brother A took him up on the bet. So Brother B went down to the bank and bought the million-pound bank note. Then the two brothers sat by the window and waited for the right man to show up.

They saw many honest faces that didn't seem smart enough. They saw many that looked smart, but not honest. Some seemed honest and smart—but not poor enough. There was always something wrong—until I came along. They decided that I filled the bill.

I didn't know what they wanted, but one of them gave me an envelope. He said there was a letter in it that would explain everything. I started to open it, but he said not to. He said to wait until I got home.

I was angry. I thought maybe they were playing a joke on me. When I got outside, I was ready to pick up the pear and eat it. But it was gone.

As soon as I was out of sight of the brothers' house, I opened the envelope. Right off, I saw that it contained money. I didn't bother to see how much the bank note was worth. I stuffed it in my pocket and headed for a restaurant.

How I did eat! When I couldn't hold any more, I took out the bill and unfolded it. I nearly fainted. That £1,000,000 bill was worth about $5 million in American money!

When the restaurant owner came with the check, I showed him the bank note. "Bring me change, please," I said.

He looked stunned. When he recovered, he apologized for not being able to break the bill.

"I must insist," I said. "Please change it, because I don't have anything smaller."

He said that was all right. I could pay him the next time I came in. I said that I might not be back in the neighborhood for some time. He said that was all right, too. He would trust a rich gentleman like me to pay him later.

I started back toward the brothers' house. I wanted to see them before they called the police. I was sure they had made a mistake. Surely they thought they were giving me a one-pound note—not one for a million pounds! It wasn't my fault, but I wanted to clear up the problem before I got into trouble.

The same butler answered the door. When I asked for the two gentlemen, he said, "They are gone."

"Gone where?" I asked.

"On a trip."

"But where?" I asked.

"I think to Europe," he said.

"When will they be back?" I asked.

"In a month," he said.

"A month!" I said. "This is awful. Give me some idea how I can get in touch with them."

"I can't," he said. "There is no way to know where they are."

"Then I must see some other family members," I said.

"The family's away, too," the butler said.

"But there's been a big mistake made," I said.

"They told me you'd come back," he said. "They said to tell you it's all right. They will be back on time."

Then I left. What a riddle it was! What did he mean, "back on time?"

Then I remembered the letter. I took it out and read it. This is what it said:

"*You are a smart and honest man, as one may see by your face. I saw that you are also poor and a stranger in London. The money in this envelope is yours for thirty days. Report to this house at that time. I have a bet on you. If I win it, you can*

have any job that I am able to give you—
if you are able to do it."

It wasn't signed and there was no address or date.

What a situation to be in! *You* know what had gone before. But at the time, I didn't. It was still a deep, dark puzzle to me.

I sat down on a park bench and thought about it. After an hour, this is what I decided:

Maybe those men mean well, and maybe they don't. All I know is that there's a bet on me. I'll let it go at that and make my own plans. If I try to get change for this bank note from the Bank of England, they'll know where it came from. But they'll think I stole it. If I tell them the truth, they'll put me in a mental hospital. The same will happen if I try to deposit it in any other bank. I've got to carry it with me until the two men get back. I've got to suffer for a month without pay—unless I help win that bet. Then it will be worth it. Men of their sort can offer jobs that are worth having.

I got to thinking a lot about that job. My hopes began to rise. Without doubt, the salary would be large. The job would begin in a month, and after that I would be all right. Pretty soon I was feeling first-rate.

I was walking the streets again when I came to a tailor shop. Could I afford some new clothes? No, I had no money, except for the million pounds. I forced myself to keep going. But I found myself drifting back again. The temptation was strong. I must have gone back and forth six times. At last I gave in. I had to.

I went into the shop and asked if they had any misfit suits—suits they were going to throw out. A fellow in the shop took me to the back room. He showed me a pile of rejected suits. I took the rattiest looking one in the pile. It didn't fit and it was ugly, but it was clean and new.

I said I'd take it. Then I added, "Could you wait a few days for the money? I don't have any small change on me."

He made a face. "Don't worry," he said, we can make change for any large bank note you might have."

I handed the note to him and said, "Oh, very well then. I apologize."

He took it with a smile. When he saw how large it was, the smile froze on his face.

The owner of the shop came over and said, "What's the matter?"

"Nothing," I said, "I'm just waiting for my change."

Then he looked at the bill and gave a whistle. He began to talk aloud, but as though he were talking to himself. "Sell a millionaire a suit like that? That's foolish! It will drive all the other millionaires away!"

Then *he* said to me, "Please, sir, take those things off. Here—try this shirt, this suit, these pants. You need something that a prince might wear." And he began to hand me lots of handsome, well-made clothes.

I was satisfied and said so. "But," I said, "you'll have to wait to get paid— unless you can change this bill." I held up the million-pound note.

He said he didn't mind waiting at all. And why should he. He thought for sure that I was rich. He was glad to get my business, even if it meant waiting awhile to get paid.

Well, don't you see what was bound to happen? I began going to other stores and buying whatever I wanted. At stores, restaurants, hotels, everyone was glad to wait. Word spread throughout the city. People even *forced* me to borrow money from them.

I was living like the rich and the great. Of course I knew the crash must come. Still, I was having such a good time, I didn't worry much about it.

My name started showing up in all the newspapers. In one paper they called me "the vest-pocket millionaire." That's because I carried the million-pound note in my vest pocket. I was becoming famous. All over town people would see me and say, "There he goes! That's him!"

I still had my ragged old suit, and every now and then I wore it. I did it for the fun of ordering something in a store.

When the clerks gave me a dirty look, I'd flash my million-pound note. Then I would watch their expressions change.

After about ten days, I was invited to a dinner party at the American Embassy in London. It turned out that the ambassador had gone to college with my father. They had been friends right up until the time my father died. He was very friendly. He told me to come around and visit whenever I could. I was willing, of course. I thought that when the crash came, he might somehow be able to save me.

I was in deep, I thought—but not *too* deep. I was borrowing a lot, but I figured I'd be able to pay it back when I was earning a salary. Of course, I didn't know what my salary would be. But I figured it would be about six hundred pounds a year. And I guessed I'd be getting raises every year. So far, I was only in debt for my first year's salary.

I'd spent about three hundred pounds on meals, lodging, and the things I'd bought. The other three hundred pounds was borrowed money that I hadn't spent. I believed my second year's salary would get me through until the end of the month. By then the brothers would be back.

The ambassador's party was a lovely dinner for fourteen people. The Duke and Duchess of Shoreditch and their daughter were there. I met the Earl and Countess of Newgate and Lord and Lady Blatherskite. Some people without titles were there, too. The ambassador's daughter had invited her friend, an English girl of twenty-two. Her name was Portia Langham. I fell in love with her in two minutes, and she with me.

There was another guest, too—an American. The butler announced his name, "Mr. Lloyd Hastings." A minute later, Hastings walked over to me. "Don't I know you?" he asked.

"You do, old fellow," I said. "I'm Henry Adams from the Hopkins Stock Brokerage in San Francisco."

"No," he said. "Aren't *you* the—the—"

"The vest-pocket millionaire?" I said.

"I am, indeed. Don't be afraid to call me by my nickname. I'm used to it."

"Well, well, Henry," he said, "this is a surprise. Just six months ago you helped me with the Gould and Curry Mine deal. I wanted you to come to London with me to finish it—do you remember? But you said you didn't think the deal would go through. And you said you were too busy to come to London. And yet here you are. How odd it all is! How did you happen to come here? And what *did* give you such a great start?"

"Oh, it was just an accident," I said. "It's a long story—a romance, you might say. I'll tell you all about it at the end of the month."

"But that's more than two weeks away," he said. "Make it a week."

"I can't," I said. "You'll know my reasons, by and by. But tell me—how is the Gould and Curry deal going?"

His cheerfulness vanished like a breath. He said with a sigh, "You were right, Henry. I wish I hadn't come. I don't want to talk about it."

"But you *must*," I said. "After dinner we'll go to my hotel. Then you can tell me all about it."

His eyes got wet. "Oh, thank you!" he said. "I've been through so much. I do need to tell someone about it."

The dinner wasn't very good, but Miss Langham and I had a lovely time. We played cards after dinner, and we talked and talked. I told her I loved her. She blushed till her hair turned red, but she liked it. She *said* she did.

I couldn't pay attention to my cards. I kept saying things like, "My, how sweet you do look!"

She would answer, "Do you think so?"

Oh, there was never such an evening.

I was perfectly honest with her. I told her I hadn't a cent in the world—just the million-pound note. And I told her that it didn't really belong to me. I talked low, so the others wouldn't hear. I told her the whole story. She nearly died laughing.

I couldn't see why she thought it was so funny. But as I talked, I would often have to stop for as much as a minute. It would take that long for her to stop laughing and settle down. Why, she laughed herself lame—she did, indeed.

I never saw a painful story have that kind of effect before. That made me love her all the more. I saw that she could be cheerful in the face of trouble. Soon I might need that kind of wife, I thought.

I told her we would have to wait a couple of years to get married. By then I'd be caught up on my salary. But she didn't mind. She only hoped I wouldn't spend too much. She didn't want me to cut into my third year's salary.

Then she began to get a little worried. She wondered if maybe I hadn't made a mistake about how high my salary would be. Maybe, she said, I'd get less the first year than I had thought.

That showed good sense, although it worried me a little. But it gave me a good idea. "Portia, dear," I said, "would you mind going along with me the day I see the brothers?"

For a moment she held back a little. Then she said, "No, I wouldn't mind. If it would help you, I'll do it. But do you think it would be proper?"

"No, I don't know that it would," I said. "In fact, I'm afraid it wouldn't. But I'd just like to have you there—"

"Then I'll go," she said. "Oh, I shall be so happy to think that I am helping!"

"Helping?" I said. "Why, you'll be doing it all. You're so beautiful and so lovely, those old fellows won't be able to resist. I'll get a huge salary from them!"

That put me in a very good mood. You may judge my mood by this fact: on the spot I raised my yearly salary to twelve hundred pounds. But I didn't tell her. I saved it for a surprise.

Later, Hastings and I walked to my hotel. He talked all the way, but I didn't listen. All I could think of was Portia.

When we got to the hotel, he said, "Look at this place. It's like a palace! It makes me realize how rich you are. But it also makes me realize how poor I am— and how unhappy and defeated!"

That scared me. It made me think of what a thin crust I was standing on—and what a big hole there was below. I hadn't allowed myself to think much about it before. But *now*—oh, dear! I was deep in debt with not a cent in the world. And a lovely girl's happiness depended on me. All I had ahead of me was a salary that I might not get!

I said to Lloyd, "Tell me your story again."

"Again?" he said.

"The whole thing," I said, because I hadn't listened to a word of it the first time.

"All right," he said. Then he told me that he had worked hard on the Gould and Curry deal for months. He was supposed to sell a gold mine to some men in London. Anything over a million dollars, he could keep for himself. But he had to sell it by the end of the month. Now it looked like the deal wasn't going to go through. All the time and money he had spent arranging the deal would be wasted.

He had worked hard, but now it looked like he would be ruined.

Suddenly he cried out, "Henry, you can save me! You're the only man in the world who can. Will you do it?"

"Tell me how," I said. "Speak out, my friend."

"Give me the million dollars for the company. It's worth much more than that—but at least I'll get *some* of my money back."

I was right at the point of saying, "Lloyd, I'm poor, too. I'm without a cent and in *debt*." But then a white-hot idea came flaming through my head. I waited for a moment to calm myself down. Then I said, "I will save you, Lloyd—"

"Then I'm already saved!" he said. "If ever I—"

"Let me finish," I said. "I will save you—but not in that way. That wouldn't be fair to you after all the hard work you've done. I know the mine is worth more than a million dollars. I want you to set a price of three million dollars for it. Then I'll tell anyone who asks that it's worth it. We'll divide the extra two million between us."

"I may use your name?" he said. "Your name—just think of it! Every rich person in London will want to buy the mine if *you* recommend it! My fortune is made. I'll never forget you as long as I live!"

In less than twenty-four hours, business people all over London were talking about the mine. People came to my hotel to ask me about it, and about Lloyd.

"Yes," I told them, "he is an honest man. And the mine is worth even more than he's asking for it."

I continued to spend all my evenings with Portia. I didn't say a word to her about the mine. I saved it for a surprise. We talked about salary—salary and love. Sometimes love, sometimes salary, sometimes love and salary together.

Lloyd sold the mine for three million and gave me my share. When the month was up, I had a million dollars in the bank. I took Portia with me to see the two brothers. On the way there we talked some more about salary. She looked beautiful!

"I've decided on the salary," I said. "I won't take a penny less than three thousand pounds a year."

"Henry, Henry," she said, "you'll ruin us!"

"Don't be afraid," I said. "Just keep those beautiful looks and trust in me. It will all come out all right, I promise you."

"Please remember," she said, "if you ask for too much, you may get no salary at all. Then what will become of us, with no way in the world to earn our living?"

The butler met us at the door. He took us in to see the two brothers. Of course they were surprised to see the wonderful creature who was with me. I told them, "She is my future wife." Then I introduced them to her, and called them by name. It didn't surprise them. They knew that I would know enough to find out who they were.

Then I said, "Gentlemen, I am ready to report."

"We are glad to hear it," said the brother who had bet on me. "Now we can decide the bet. If you have won it for me—you can have any job that I can give. Have you the million-pound note?"

"Here it is, sir," I said. Then I handed it to him.

"I've won!" he shouted. He slapped the other man on the back. "What do you say to that, brother?"

The other brother said, "I say! He *did* survive after all! And I've lost twenty thousand pounds. I never would have believed it."

"I've got more to tell," I said. "Take a look at this." I took out my bankbook and showed them that I had a million dollars in the bank.

Portia gasped. "Henry," she said, "is that *really* your money? Have you been fibbing to me?"

"I have indeed, dear," I said. "But you'll forgive me, I know."

"Oh, don't be so sure," she said. "You are a naughty thing to fool me so!"

"You'll get over it, sweetheart," I said. "You'll get over it. It was only in fun, you know. Come, let's be going."

"But wait, wait!" the brother who had bet on me said, "The job, you know. I want to give you the job."

"Well, thank you," I said, "but really I don't want a job now."

"But you can have the best job I have to offer!" he cried.

"Thanks again, with all my heart," I said, "but I don't even want that."

"Henry, I'm ashamed of you," Portia said. "You haven't thanked the good gentlemen half enough. May I do it for you?"

"Indeed, you shall, my dear," I said, "Go ahead."

She went to my man and put her arm around his neck. Then she kissed him right on the mouth. The two old gentlemen shouted with laughter, but I was shocked!

Then Portia said, "Papa, he says you don't have anything he wants. I feel just as hurt as—"

"My darling," I said. "Is that your papa?"

"Yes," Portia said. "He's my stepfather—and the dearest one that ever was. Now you know why I was able to laugh when you first told me about the bank note."

Of course, I spoke up right away. Without any fooling, I went straight to point. "Sir, I want to take back what I said. You do have a job that I want."

"Name it," he said.

"Son-in-law," I said.

"Well, well, well!" he said. "But if you haven't held that job before, you have no experience. You have no proof that you can do it."

"Try me!" I said. "Oh, do, I beg of you! Just try me for thirty or forty years, and if—"

"Oh, well, all right," he laughed. "It's but a little thing to ask. Take her along."

Were we two happy! There are not words enough to describe it. And when the people in London heard the whole story, did they have a good time? Yes, indeed.

I owe everything I have to the £1,000,000 note that I never spent. It gave me my Portia. Without it I never would have met her at the ambassador's dinner. I always say, "It was a million-pounder, but it only bought one thing. And what it got me was worth about ten times that much!"

A Fable

Can you always believe your own eyes? The other animals thought they could trust the cat—but now they think he's lying. After they check out his story, they're even more confused.

"THE CAT LIED. THERE WAS NOTHING IN THAT
HOLE BUT A DONKEY."

A Fable

Once upon a time, an artist painted a very small and very beautiful picture. He placed it so that he could see it in a mirror. "This doubles the distance and softens it," he said. "Now it is twice as lovely as before."

The woodland animals heard about the picture from the artist's cat. They admired the cat. They thought that he was very polite and refined and civilized. Because he was so smart and highbred, he could tell them about things they didn't understand.

When they asked what a picture was, the cat explained.

"It is a flat, smooth thing," the cat said. "It's wonderfully flat, marvelously flat and elegant. In every way, it's oh, so beautiful!"

That excited the other animals. They said that they would give the world to see it.

Then the cow spoke up. "What is a mirror?" she asked.

"It is a hole in the wall," said the cat. "When you look in it, you see the picture. And the picture is so dainty and charming that it turns your head round and round. You almost faint from happiness."

The donkey had doubts. He didn't think the picture could be as beautiful as the cat said it was. "Why do you need such a basket of words to praise a thing of beauty?" he said.

That made the cat mad, and he left.

The other animals weren't sure who was right.

The donkey said there was only one

way to find out. He would go and see for himself.

When he got to the artist's room, he didn't know where to stand. By mistake he stood between the picture and the mirror. Of course, he could not see the reflection of the picture.

The donkey went right back to the woodland. "The cat lied," he said to the animals. "There was nothing in that hole but a donkey. To be sure, it was a nice, friendly donkey. But it was just a donkey, and nothing more."

The elephant, who was King of the Beasts, said, "The cat never lied before. I think another of us should go and look in the hole. That way we can be sure."

This time the bear went. When he came back he said, "Both the cat and the donkey lied. There was nothing in the hole but a bear."

The elephant sent the other animals one at a time.

The cow found nothing in the hole but a cow.

The tiger found nothing in it but

a tiger.

The camel found a camel and nothing more.

At last, the elephant went to see for himself. When he came back, he was angry. He said they were all liars. For certain, he said, there was nothing in the hole but an elephant.

MORAL, BY THE CAT

What you can find in a picture or a book depends on you. You will find whatever you bring to it—if you stand between it and the mirror of your imagination. You may not see your ears, but they will be there.

Thinking About
the Stories

The Celebrated Jumping Frog of
Calaveras County

1. All stories fit into one or more categories. Is this story serious or funny? Would you call it an adventure, a love story, or a mystery? Is it a character study? Or is it simply a picture the author has painted of a certain time and place? Explain your thinking.

2. Good writing always has an effect on the reader. How did you feel when you finished reading this story? Were you surprised, sad, horrified, amused, touched, or inspired? What elements in the story made you feel that way?

3. An author builds the plot around the conflict in a story. In this story, what forces or characters are struggling against each other? How is the conflict finally resolved?

The Californian's Tale

1. What period of time is covered in this story—an hour, a week, several years? What role, if any, does time play in the story?

2. Are there friends or enemies in this story? Who are they? What forces do you think keep the friends together and the enemies apart?

3. Did the story plot change direction at any point? Explain the turning point of the story.

The Professor's Yarn

1. Interesting story plots often have unexpected twists and turns. What surprises did you find in this story?

2. Who is the main character in this story? Who are one or two of the minor characters? Describe each of these characters in one or two sentences.

3. All the events in a story are arranged in a certain order, or sequence. Tell about one event from the beginning of this story, one from the middle, and one from the end. How are these events related?

The Million-Pound Bank Note

1. In what town, city, or country does this story take place? Is the location important to the story? Why or why not?

2. The plot is the series of events that takes place in a story. Usually, story events are linked in some way. Can you name an event in this story that was the cause of a later event?

3. Compare and contrast at least two characters in this story. In what ways are they alike? In what ways are they different?

A Fable

1. Look back at the illustration that introduces this story. What character or characters are pictured? What is happening in the scene? What clues does the picture give you about the time and place of the story?

2. Many stories are meant to teach a lesson of some kind. Is the author trying to make a point in this story? What is it?

3. What is the title of this story? Can you think of another good title?